The Journey through Cancer

(How to Lose 25 pounds without diet or exercise!! Cancer Free in 8 Months)

Author:
Jim Serritella
Caregiver
Advocate
Guardian
Listener

First published by Dog Ear Publishing
4011 Vincennes Rd
Indianapolis, IN 46268
www.dogearpublishing.net

ISBN: 978-1-4575-4625-9

This book is printed on acid-free paper.

Printed in the United States of America

A Dedication

To my wife and best friend, Elizabeth, I Love You!

To our son, Vincent - you are my best buddy and I could only have done this with your help. Love Dad

To my dearest friends,
Judy Bretz , Gerry O'Brien,
and Craig "Metal" Meyer
who lost their battles with cancer.
And to all who went before us to establish
this process of recovery from cancer.
I write this in your loving memory.
Thank you!

Endorsements

#1   Daniel Grey – Attorney – Cancer Survivor

#2   Nancy P. – Shihan – Multiple Cancer Survivor

#3   Dr. Neil Farber – MD - Author

#4   Dr. J. Garrett Reilly – MD – Oncologist

#5   Dr. Paul Bannen – MD – Oncologist

#6   Alan Goldberg – Sifu – Publisher

#1   March 11, 2016

Dear Jim,

I met you just before my own cancer journey started. Unfortunately, my Stage III lymph cancer beginning in October 2013 prevented me from working for several months, but my cancer ordeal enabled me to give you and Betty benefit of a few items, one of which is the need for an over-the-counter antacid for the stomach just after chemo, so one can tie on the old feed bag.

I was very moved reading the entire manuscript, and as you note, the patient and his/her family and friends cannot ask enough questions. I was stunned when my oncologist and her nurses told me most patients don't seem all that interested in the details of the cancer battle they are fighting, but Jim and Liz handled the challenge properly, wanting to understand their challenge, and prepare themselves spiritually and emotionally for their journey. Jim's anecdotes about the Crosses in Life, the Marbles on Saturday, and the "I Wish You Enough" from the father to his daughter, are all lessons we need to re-learn to understand the preciousness of life, and the importance of conveying our love to others when they most need it, and not when it's convenient for us.

What most affected me during my six chemo sessions of seven to eight hours every three weeks, was seeing the suffering of patients in far worse shape than I was, which moved me to constant silent prayer in their presence, and made my heart yearn to help them, even though I can be a grumpy-sort at times. Jim's concern for Liz during his diary is manifest, as is patience with the two Labs/Border Collies, who needed an hour and a half of this time to "be happy", even when he didn't arrive home to spend time with them until 11:30 PM. When reading the manuscript, when Liz came down to

Thanksgiving dinner to join Vince, Stephanie and Jim, I remembered my own first cancer Thanksgiving, when my doctors let me go to my brother's house to join my family for dinner, and I walked in the door and all the people present applauded me being there, which made me go out and walk the dog, a Jim Serritella reaction, as I was so overcome.

My treatment and remission scan occurred in late April 2014, and I remember getting the good news a day after the scan, and going to I-Hop in Falls Church, VA as I had an old-fashioned midday brunch craving, proving my returned good health. Jim and Liz began their journey six weeks later, and I was able to brief him on what it was like, although Liz had a far more challenging process due to the radiation, and the 103 degree fever. I was praying for Liz and her family and friends constantly after Jim disclosed her condition, and I well remember how they were fired up about their St. Lucia trip for their 37th anniversary. Many memories about Liz's condition over this stretch came back to me, as I reviewed the narrative.

This book offers great spiritual, medical and practical guidance for the cancer patient, caregiver, relative of patient, friend of patient, and those working on the patient's prayer chain. Please read it, and remember how each of us being treated need those daily naps, good nights of sleep, and the knowledge that our loved ones are in our corner at all times, supporting our effort to battle the disease, with prayer, good wishes, humor and the occasional good meal.

Cancer Survivor - Daniel M. Gray, Attorney at Law, Falls Church, VA

#2

Jim........Not sure I'm kicking cancer's butt, but my tumor markers have come down significantly! The man upstairs has certainly been testing me to extreme limits. Cancer is a battle and you enter armed and ready OR surrender immediately! I have never been graceful at quitting anything, so I will continue to fight in the hopes that this will be a First Place Event for me. I feel, The Journey is a book written for me highlighted by the questions I've asked of all my doctors. I loved the epilog.

Shihan Nancy P. is multiple cancer survivor over the last 5 years. She is a 7th degree black belt in "Yoshitsune Ju Jutsu" with 43 years experience in martial arts. She lives on Long Island, NY.

#3

The Journey is a heartfelt personal account of struggle through the diagnosis, treatment and recovery of cancer. This book is not an oncology textbook written by a medical expert. This is a user's guide written by an experienced caregiver intended to help other patients, caregivers and "team members" get a better understanding and insight into this most challenging process.

Dr. Neil Farber, MD, PhD, Associate. Professor - Anesthesiology, Pediatrics, Pharmacology & Toxicology (retired). Adjunct Professor Psychology, Arizona State University, Author, Making Lemonade: 101 Recipes to Convert Negatives into Positives.

#4

J. Garrett Reilly, M.D., Ph.D., F.A.CP.

Medical Oncology and Hematology
3418 Olandwood Ct., Suite 111
Olney, MD 20832
Phone: 301-774-8198 Fax: 301-774-8199

James Serritella
8004 Hilton Road
Laytonsville, MD 20882
February 21, 2016

Dear Mr. Serritella

Thank you for the opportunity the review the manuscript, "The Journey", which chronicles your wife's experiences with lung cancer. For most patients this journey from diagnosis to possible cure has many unique twists and turns. The current individualized therapy that are available make this process confusing and overwhelming for patients. I was impressed how you and your wife faced these hurdles and continued to persevere. Documenting how you and your wife dealt with these obstacles was part of the process of dealing with the disease. This manuscript provides a means for closure with the disease. It also offers to the novice a way of understanding the disease. It will also provide insight into some of the steps involved with dealing with a cancer.

It is always a pleasure to read about how different people deal with the complexity and the multiple step involved in cancer treatment. Remarkably this journey is not just for the patient alone; the spouse, family, friends and the medical team all become involved. We all share in the joy of success as well as the sadness when the therapy is unsuccessful. I would hope that others would benefit by reading about your wife's experiences.

Sincerely;

J. Garrett Reilly, M.D., Ph.D., F.A.C.P.

#5

Community Hematology Oncology Practitioners

18111 Prince Philip Drive Suite #327

Olney, MD 20832

Phone: (301) 774-6136 Fax: (301) 570-0136

To Whom It May Concern,

It is with great pleasure that I am writing and endorsing the publication " *The Journey— how to lose 25 pounds without diet or exercise!! Cancer free in 8 months."* As a treating oncologist, it is always interesting and enlightening to read about cancer from the patient's perspective. Even though I was seeing Betty Serritella regularly during the treatment of her cancer, I still learned many new things by reading about her experiences. The diagnosis of cancer is certainly a journey, and I believe that a writing such as this helps not only patients who are newly diagnosed, but also their families and friends. I appreciate the candor of the book, and recommended this for newly diagnosed cancer patients, and their families.

Sincerely,

Paul Bannen, M.D.

Paul Bannen 4/7/2016

Signed By:

Paul Bannen MD

#6

April 12, 2016

A book endorsement for *"The Journey through Cancer – how to lose 25 pounds without diet or exercise. And be cancer free in 8 months."*

I have known Betty and Jim Serritella for over 10 years supplying quality martial arts embroidery to our industry and sport throughout the world. When the news became known Betty had lung cancer, my team at Action Martial Arts Magazine and I phoned Betty to express our fight and determination on beating this disease. It was caught early enough to allow the doctors time to develop a plan to be cancer free. I sensed a level of anxiety and uncertainty, but the will to win was still part of her composure and determination.

This book is the path to beating cancer. It gives the patient and family an even chance at winning. Questions are essential, focus and direction are the compass to success. Betty and Jim had the necessary ingredients to beat cancer. AND they did! Cancer is a team sport.

I highly recommend *The Journey* to anyone going through cancer at any stage. This is your blueprint, get your doctor to read it, and together you will increase your success rate. Martial arts is a repetitive process of practice and tests to advance in the respect of the art. Medical progress is the result of years of practice to achieve large strides in beating diseases. Together you will win!

Sifu Alan Goldberg
Action Martial Arts Magazine – publisher
47 years - 9th dan Hall of Honors
New York, New York

Table of Contents

The Journey Begins!

Preface

"How to Lose 25 Pounds Without Diet or Exercise" sounds like a dream for most people who would like to trim a few pounds. The reality, however, is being in poor health that then generates its own weight loss program—and you will not be a happy camper going through the process. This book is the story of going through and surviving excruciating Stage 3A lung cancer. It is a remarkable story that began by accident after an uncontrollable upset stomach in the emergency room of our local hospital, MedStar Montgomery (formally Montgomery General Hospital – Montgomery, Maryland). Welcome to the journey of fighting and beating Stage 3A lung cancer.

For those of you experiencing potential problems which *may* be cancer-related, regardless of which organ—lung, breast, stomach, prostrate, etc.—know this primary rule: Got questions? Talk to the doctor! There is another section of *The Journey* regarding the rules of the game, known as The Process. Your doctors' help define the process. The Process works…follow it!

There are three parts to this book. You will see what part is best for you as you read it. A light may turn on, or you will want to remember that fact later. Whatever it is, it is part of your journey through this ordeal.

Welcome to *The Journey*—an experience—and hopefully a lesson learned to help others. And a special thanks to Bob Perks for permission to include "I Wish You Enough" material and to the Yogi Berra Museum for permission to use a Yogi Berra quote.

Also, thank you to Fabrications - graphics and designs, LLC (www.fabrications.us) - Ms. Marty Williams for the editorial and graphic support in getting "The Journey" to press.

Sincerely,

Betty & Jim Serritella
Laytonsville, Maryland

"When you come to a fork in the road, take it."
—Yogi Berra

Introduction

*T*he *Journey through Cancer* is not written in the typical third-person point of view or even in a narrative of a particular situation or event. *The Journey* is real life and is written in first-person and second-person, singular and plural involvement of the issue at hand—lung cancer (or your particular kind of cancer). YOU have a major activity and/or resultant in the discussion. Because my wife of thirty-seven years, Betty, is the primary person throughout the book and I am the writer of the story, the tense and wording are factual and to the point. You are here, and I want you to realize The Journey is real—because we lived it, and you are, or may be, living it. Cancer is a rotten disease, regardless of where it occurs in the body. It can be treated, and it can be beaten given the right parameters. I hope your introduction to *The Journey* is educational and provides an emersion into being a patient, advocate, or caregiver. *The Journey* is a team effort. We went through it together, we are winners, and my wife is the survivor. I am part of the support cast of thousands. Get your team to read *The Journey through Cancer.*

This introduction establishes and presents the players or team members, the problem (lung cancer), the suggestive methods of curing and removing the cancer, and the road map of The Journey (the process). The doctors are consultants. They illustrate and suggest, and you may accept their rationale and suggestions. Pack your bag of patience, join the road show of medical progress, and do not take anything for granted. Welcome to the world of change!!

Doctors will say, "The tumor has changed. *why?* We need to apply a different medication." Your question may or may not be answered. *why?* Things change in the blink of an eye. There are more than thirty definitions of the word "change." The three categories of "change" include: verb used with an object, verb used without an object, and noun. The reality of the word can be reduced to seven major categories.

1. Change happens to everyone and everything. Nothing is constant except death—and then you change to ashes!
2. You can wait for change and wait for the results of a prior action or activity.
3. While waiting for change, you can monitor the activity of a test or process.
4. Upon seeing the results, swift corrective action may be necessary when noticing a change pattern.
5. Take the action needed once change occurs.
6. After the change, continue to be speculative, but relish the change.
7. And, once more, after the change, stand vigil to change again.

As you make your way through *The Journey* and this book, be ready to adapt and change as many times as needed in monitoring the medical process or procedures. This book will present and comment on these change activities.

"Go see your doctor"

CHAPTER 1

The Examination Accident

So you have an upset stomach. You really have an upset stomach—as in you vomit several times in a short period of time. My car or the car with the flashing lights and sirens—no decision there, no time to waste—the ambulance arrived and we're off to the emergency room. Upon examination and after testing and results, my wife had a urinary tract infection (UTI) which substantially disrupted her digestive tract. Medicines were prescribed. Women are more frequently affected by UTI problems. Let's take a chest x-ray to see if you have any form of lung congestion, blockage, or respiratory irritation. The results were simple, the sentence easily stated, and the next time period of life was about to be defined: "No pneumonia, but there is a white spot on the top right lung. You better have your doctor look at this!!"

And with that sentence life needed definition and direction. We knew it was not related to the UTI. Upon a visit to our primary doctor, a CT scan was prescribed and further definition was presented. A few days later, the object is a mass of growth the size of a golf ball. A further scan was needed to define the mass' contents. Sometimes these examination sites are near each other; in our case, another day of travel, scheduling, and going through the test—twenty minutes. Leave and wait for the call of the results, probably the next day.

This chapter could be much longer. I have shortened it to make a definitive point of participation, location, and to identify the players. The examination is the source of the event exercises. The members of the support staff are presented in the next chapter, The Team.

The symptoms of a disease vary—a cough, an itchy place on the skin, frequent urination, etc. First an examination, a test or tests, and a determination of the problem. Ultimately, the goal is to get to a corrective action: stop the cough, use a cream on the skin, and relieve a disruptive bladder. Don't stop asking questions and always confer with your doctors. Again, be patient. The test may take a day or two. In this world of instant gratification, sometimes "instant" is an extra day or two to mix the right formula for the magic potion.

Take heed: the team wins this battle! We all collectively show up and cheer on the result, findings, and accomplishments. Collectively, we feel the sigh of defeat where test results are not what was expected. Meet the team.

Weathering the storm!

CHAPTER 2

The Team

At all times the applicable team doctors must confer with each other. In the past, they called and spoke with each other. Today, more than not, communication is an electronic message or report being forwarded to the participating doctor. Do not take any doctor for granted. Contrary to popular belief, the doctor works for you. If you are not comfortable with your doctor, stop the process, go back to your primary doctor, relay your situation and status, and request a new whomever: "Get me another doctor please." In the position of guardian, I have had one doctor removed from my wife's case and questioned, with definitive results, a doctor's approach and diagnosis with positive action defined by myself and agreed to by our attending physician.

THE TEAM....Who, What, Where, When, Why

Your primary doctor is your key member of the team until he turns you over to the oncologist and Radiation-oncologist. Then material and information flows from the specialists to your primary doctor for follow-up activities. Our team for this effort, right lung cancer, is comprised of eight doctors of different specialties and their supporting staff.

Build yourself a contact sheet of names, activities, phone numbers, locations, fax numbers, and e-mail addresses. Keep business cards. If you are proficient in making spreadsheets, now is the time to do so.

I have provided our skeletal team. Their information has been left off intentionally.

The team includes:

- Dr........., Director of Internal Medicine
- Dr........., Head of Oncology
- Dr........., Director of Cancer Radiology
- Dr........., NCI (National Cancer Institute of Pathology – Bethesda, MD)
- Dr........., Head of Thoracic Surgery (Holy Cross Hospital – Silver Spring, MD)
- Dr........., Head of Pulmanology Department – Silver Spring, MD
- Dr........., Head of Department of Immunology & Microbiology at N.I.H.
- Dr........., Pulmonologist – Lung specialist for ongoing measurement and status checks
- SrRN........., Senior registered nurses, technicians, and support staff relevant to the administration of numerous test, port flushing, and chemo/radiology procedures
- The Watchdog team (in our case a single person, me):
  - A Guardian
  - A Caretaker
  - An Advocate
  - A Spokesperson
  - An Approver

Did you ever get the feeling you're herding cats? You need to be organized and keep track of doctors' directions, medication dosages and time-frames, examination or testing locations, etc. I suggest a bound tablet of paper for note taking and patient specifics.

This is essential information: get to know the receptionists by name and always be cordial. Continue to exhibit confidence. There will be days of "I really don't want to be here," but crack a smile anyway.

Have everything explained—twice if you need it – take notes. Why do they call it stage 3A? Oh, that incorporates these tests? The tests and their results define the number and the stage. It may be minutia to you, but the reality is THERE IS a process to the definition and specific treatment of the stage and involved organ.

The more you ask, the better you will be able to understand and update The Journey for someone else. As a caretaker, tell the doctors what you are doing at home. Should I be doing something else in a different way? Any special foods we should be eating? Should the patient be using the steps at home? Any particular symptoms I should be looking for before I call you (the doctor or his designee)? On and on… keep asking.

Very important point here: One of our doctors is Dr………, NCI (National Cancer Institute of Pathology – Bethesda, MD). You need to know about this. You, as a tax-paying individual with a serious medical problem, can use the resources of the NCI for information related to your cancer. They are most helpful and will discuss numerous options for you to present to your doctor and support team. They will offer information on various medical conditions and clinical trials or tests applicable to your cancer. In our case, we substantiated the cancer value of 3A to determine and re-establish from our local pathology that, in fact, we are treating a cancer patient with a 3A lung cancer disease. Keep asking questions. You will get to the right approach for your patient. Thank you, Dr….., NCI.

Do *not* lose your sense of humor in this battle. It is needed to reinforce the level of comedy required to meet the problem head-on. And of all the players, you have to meet and greet the team chemo supporter assisted by functional gravity, a true stand-up piece of equipment needed for each chemo session.

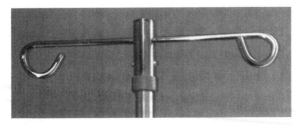

Sir Ralph at your service: You hang 'em, gravity drains 'em—glad to help!

This IV pole stand plays an important part in your cancer treatment. "Sir Ralph" represents a level of humor in this entire cancer journey. A perfect example: We had already purchased a wig anticipating my wife's hair loss. A few weeks later, while I was sitting in the kitchen of our home, my wife comes into the kitchen after awakening in the bedroom. I took one look at her, and in a louder than normal voice I said, "Go get the wig!" We both laughed, and she ruffled and tried to straighten her hair. During the eight months, there were several forced comedy situations, I'll leave those up to you, but don't stop laughing at each other and at the problem. At times the tension gets a little too heavy. Clear the air of the tension and have a cup of coffee together. You have to get back on the right track—together!!

In presenting the team to you, I address a subject seldom presented in any cancer publication: THE COST OF CANCER TREATMENT. The drugs—all the drugs—, the chemotherapy, the radiation treatments, and whatever else is needed to support the patient are expensive. Some patients have medical insurance; other people have minimal or no insurance. (I will not address anything related to the Affordable Healthcare Act [more commonly known as "Obamacare"] as I am not sure what it covers.)

Our insurance covered some of the costs, yet there still was a substantial amount to be paid for doctors, hospitals, and supporting services. I do not know if there are grants for assistance payments to help treat and pay for a patient's care. The attending doctors may help secure financial patient assistance. Contact the American Cancer Society for additional details.

In discussing this subject in a business environment with cancer physicians, there are doctors who are true to the medical oath of helping others—there is nothing in the oath regarding fees or payments. Each case is different, and each doctor or organization is different as to how they conduct their business. I applaud the doctors who have expressed themselves in discussing their services. Medical practices are businesses also. They are meant to be profitable and self-supporting for the employees and employer. Sometimes the profit margin is not as large as it could be. AMEN!

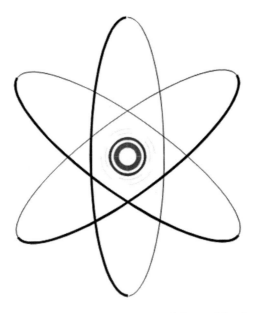

The atom is the solution ... and the problem?

CHAPTER 3

The Problem

I n the world of problems, analysis, and solutions, questions must be asked to derive the proper approach toward the overall end. In this case, the PROBLEM is presented before the QUESTIONS so that the depth of the issue can be assessed first. Some of the recommended questions follow this section.

At all times the doctors are cautious in the discussions—noncommittal and constantly needing more data. At all points along this road, there is frustration. "What if" comments abound. And why does it take so long?

Now a thoracic surgeon is involved to prescribe the next scan, a PT scan: nuclear based, contrast injection with "stuff" needed. It takes 45 minutes to complete. The chest doctor and primary doctor agree—a biopsy is needed. The PT scan has included chest lymph nodes which appear to be part of the problem. More questions arise.

Additional time is being taken. Now a conference with a pulmonologist and thoracic doctors must include operating room coordination for dates and availability time. Days go by; frustration is exhibited. No decision is being confirmed as to the definition of the mass and lymph.

This biopsy is a relatively new procedure: electromagnetic navigation bronchoscopy involving GPS technology with a device inserted into the esophagus. This provides the correct location, and a biopsy is taken of the lymph node(s) to be sampled for potential cancer. After the lymph(s) are sampled, the device is inserted down into the lungs and upward toward the mass shown on the CT scan location. The mass is sampled and "marked" for future radiation procedures. Two doctors executed the biopsy processes. All slides were analyzed at the local hospital and were also sent to the National Cancer Institute of Bethesda for additional analysis and diagnosis. Again, more time is needed to analyze and report to the doctors.

On this journey, there will be many battles and skirmishes. This is not a one-day event—don't blow it!! Keep cool, and the doctors will respect your demonstrations and feelings of anxiety and delays. There is travel to consider: Where is the next lab for imaging and testing? Who is responsible for reporting back to us? Do I need an office visit to obtain the test results? Questions abound!!

The examination is only the beginning. Keep a log, write down all questions for any doctor, and keep your primary doctor in the loop at all times.

And there will be problems—do not be discouraged. All problems have a reasonable solution. Find what is best for your condition.

After the biopsy, the thoracic surgeon came out and presented the process or "plan" to treat this level of cancer. The oncologist also agreed with the plan, and the first leg of the Journey began to take shape. Every cancer is different, and the majority are treatable if caught early in the game. Based on a normal timeframe with no illness or problems, our plan was as follows:

- Install a port – (formal name – indwelling intravenous catheter)
- Chemo for four treatments, spaced out every three weeks
- At the same time chemo is administered, radiation for twenty-five treatments, five consecutive days at a time (usually with the weekend days off for no treatment)

- After the four chemo and twenty-five radiation sessions, surgery to remove the cancer, lymph nodes, and lung segments as determined during the operation
- Surgical recovery time. Don't rush it—you will get better!
- Consider any adjustments to the plan. There will be delays for various reasons.

Welcome to *The Journey*. A planned approach has been established for lung cancer patients with a 3A stage—upper right lobe (remember this sentence). The itinerary requires all members of the team to be versed in flexibility and patience. *The Journey* presents the stages of the illness and the recovery broadcasts to our numerous friends, relatives, and well-wishers following the initial cancer announcement.

While the plan has been established, some preliminary steps must be accomplished prior to the actual steps to rid the body of cancer. The oncologist, the radiation-oncologist, and the patient discuss the following:

- The quantities and specific chemo compounds to be used for this cancer. The term chemo is a generic term for the process of the application of the different medications. Chemotherapy (often abbreviated to chemo and sometimes CTX or CTx) is a category of cancer treatment that uses chemical substances, especially one or more anti-cancer drugs (chemotherapeutic agents) that are given as part of a standardized chemotherapy regimen.
- When will a port be installed in the patient's body (usually the chest area)? (The port provides easy access for the chemo connection into a shoulder vein and minimizes vein discomfort in the forearm area

Picture I – Port incision
scar left front chest

due to the toxicity of the chemo compounds and associated IV solutions. The port also decreases the "drip time" needed to get the chemo solutions into the body [see Picture I].)

- Implantation of the port device by a thoracic surgeon.
- What, if any over-the-counter medications will be suggested to the patient to ease any discomfort resulting from the chemo cocktail administered every "X" weeks. (For example, the patient can take an over-the-counter antacid daily to treat acid reflux and minimize nausea.)
- Frequency of the chemo sessions, as determined by the oncologist (every three weeks, for example). The oncologist presents the sequence of the chemos and what is to be expected during the time between chemo sessions.
- The port remains in the body until the doctors agree the chemo process has been completed for the patient, at which time the patient undergoes another surgical procedure to remove the port from the body.
- While the patient is being treated with chemo, the patient cannot drink *any* alcoholic beverages. *This is very important*.
- Chemo is ultimately removed from the body through filtration by the kidney and liver. Alcohol is also filtered through the same organs. By drinking alcohol and undergoing chemo treatment at the same time, you are stressing the body's filtration organs, which will result in another compound bodily problem. REPEAT: The patient *cannot* drink alcoholic beverages while undergoing chemo.

Sounds simple, followed by some reasonable explanation. Because this is lung cancer, we, the Team (docs, et.al.), have to be sensitive to the overall condition of the patient, her lung tissue, and surrounding organs. We have to be concerned about exterior influences since it is winter time as we go through this treatment: potential flu outbursts or individuals with the flu. Between each chemo session, it was a good idea to somewhat isolate my wife and greatly minimize any external house departures. It worked, except during the second chemo session and the end of the last radiation session when she was very sick and was hospitalized again. It was a long timeframe and disrupted the original game plan of timing and positional treatment. Another UTI: serious and treatable with routine antibiotics and time. Key ingredient: TIME.

The overall schedule had to be modified. I recall one evening in the hospital as my wife was sleeping, remembering the story of the crosses of life. Why us? Why was this cancer happening to us? Well, it brings to mind the individual who constantly was having many difficulties in life and broke down and cried out to God, "WHY ME, God?" And in an unusual earthly appearance God replied, "Sir, do you agree, there must be some crosses in a person's life to warrant the suffering and pain of living on this earth before entering heaven?" The man agreed with God's statement. God replied, "I will show you the room of crosses in life—from a splinter in the finger to a paralyzed quadriplegic. You, sir, must pick out your cross of life to bear going forward. OK?" Again, the man agreed and entered the room of crosses. He spent many hours examining all the crosses one could conceivably endure in a life time. Eventually, he emerged from the room carrying a cross he thought he could manage in his lifetime. He returned to God and announced his finding. God acknowledged his cross and requested to look at it more closely before He departed. Upon examination of the cross, God said, "Sir, I notice the cross you selected happens to be the same cross I originally gave you earlier in your life." God will only give you what you can handle...with His help.

And with that came a mental awakening, knowing we are going through this experience together—God, Betty and I—and we will get through this to a successful end. We are not in control of the event. Hang on for the ride—it will be exciting.

Upon coming out of the hospital, we resumed a level of normalcy with medication, rest, small amounts of activity, and requested meals. During this time, after the second chemo session, my wife had to get her strength up in preparation for the upcoming lung surgery.

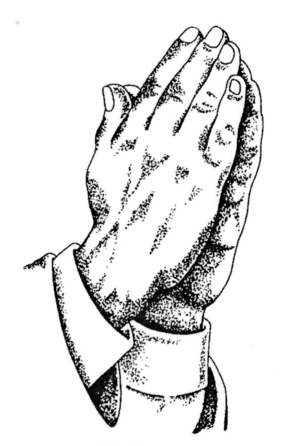

God – the answer.
Why me? – the question.

CHAPTER 4

Prayer

There is an old military expression, "There are no atheists in a foxhole." Welcome to the cancer foxhole! I don't care whether you are Catholic, Jewish, Protestant, and atheist, or whatever: you will pray to a deity or higher power. God, Yahweh, or Buddha discussions (I will use the term of God) will become part of your daily mediation and petition. It just will. Refer to any of the updates presented in Chapter 6.

"Let us remember we are in the holy presence of God, in the name of the Father, the Son, and the Holy Spirit." Anyone who has been educated by the Christian Brothers of St. John de LaSalle will know and remember the opening words to all prayers on the hour and half-hour while attending school. Followed by the closing words of the prayer: *"Live, Jesus, in our hearts forever."* The Christian Brother community had, and still has, a major influence in my life. Did we pray before exams? Of course. Have I continued to pray in times of uncertain moments in my life? Of course. And when the cancer diagnosis was announced, we prayed. And over the succeeding months of tests, appointments, treatments, and operations, we kept a prayer vigil.

You can't go through this journey alone— you need a team. We had a huge team invoking God to direct the curing process for Betty. We are practicing Catholics, and our God is an almighty God who, from the beginning of the accidental x-ray through to the declaration of "free of cancer," has been beseeched by masses to be instrumental in the ultimate revelation of "free of cancer." Our prayer team consisted of people, organizations, and unknown contributors, including:

- The St. Paul Church community (our Sunday Mass community) of Damascus, Maryland
- The Catholic Daughters of the Americas members—Betty's organization Church affiliation
- The Knights of Columbus members—my organization Church affiliation
- Our family members and friends who have said, "I'll pray for you."
- Members of America Legion Post 171, Damascus, Maryland—my legion post
- St. Patrick H.S., Chicago, Illinois—the Christian Brothers and friends
- Members of the embroidery community worldwide, who receive the updates I send out to keep the group up to date on Betty and other individuals needing prayer support
- Individuals known as "Angels"—folks who have and continue to pray for Betty as well as send us handmade sewn angels and messages of continued support
- Friends in other religious denominations who have posted Betty's name on their prayer lists
- Our friends in other parts of the world who pray to God in different tongues (as seen in Chapter 6: The Updates)
- Our prayer support team included Archbishop Anthony Obinna from Nigeria, Africa, the Owerri Province, who was visiting friends at St. Paul parish in Damascus, Maryland; priests from several religious orders; deacons; and even Pope Francis, who provided a blessing when we traveled to Rome, Italy.

In this immediate gratification society, we find it difficult to realize that God listens to prayer. The "I want it, or need it, NOW" requests are not part of God's instinctive response. You have heard many times that God listens. You have to *ask*, and He will hear you and provide whatever you ask for. Yep, "Ask and it will be given to you; seek and you will find; knock and the door will be opened to you. are the words in scripture – Matthew 7:7. The reply may not be instantaneous, or even realized by the requestor as a NOW thing. God works in strange and ubiquitous ways.

I know God has heard the many, many prayers on Betty's behalf to be rid of this terrible disease. And God has blessed us in many ways, including receiving the ultimate blessing of being cancer-free. As others have prayed for us, we too have prayed for others suffering from all forms of cancer. I know He hears us—all of us—because of the massive strides and results in curing the devil's disease. For example, there were limited types of chemo available in the 1990s, and today there are numerous improved chemo treatments, including a pill. Ultimately, we pray for the elimination of the word cancer from our society, and for the survivors of the deceased who cancer has taken from us. See chapter 10.

I can cite a very explicit personal example: My brother was diagnosed with polio in the 1950s, the day Dr. Jonas Salk discovered and released his findings that he had found the cure for polio. Today, you rarely hear of a polio case unless the individual did not get the polio vaccination. Someday, the word CANCER will be removed from our medical diagnosis. God will listen in his time. He is in control—ALWAYS.

"We cannot direct the wind, but we can adjust our sails." —old nautical saying

- Life is a gift.
- Today, before you say an unkind word, think of someone who can't speak.
- Before you complain about the taste of your food, think of someone who has nothing to eat.

- Before you complain about your husband or wife, think of someone who's crying out for a companion.
- Today, before you complain about life, think of someone who went too early to heaven.
- Before whining about the distance you drive, think of someone who walks the same distance.
- And when you are tired and complain about your job, think of the unemployed, the disabled, and those who wish they had your job.
- And when depressing thoughts seem to get you down, put a smile on your face and think: you're alive and still around.

If you don't ask, you'll never know!

CHAPTER 5

Questions—Lots of Them

W hat follows are some questions and some answers to the overall process and events. You will be enlightened as to what to expect during the journey.

What happens in a chemo session? Some chemo sessions are administered at the doctor's office; others are performed at an infusion center. Both are similar in the process, and some are decorated a little more lavishly than others. After a small greeting, you are escorted to a private room or a lounge with several reclining chairs. While you lounge in the comfortable chair, your port is medically cleaned and wiped with a medical swab, and an IV needle is placed in the port. The port is flushed (cleaned for adequate blood flow), and a blood sample is taken for immediate blood counts. White and red counts are very important to the therapy.

The chemo session for my wife's lung cancer consisted of four or five bags of medicines (partially based on blood counts) as well as the applicable medications for the desired chemo affect. The time to receive the four or five bags was almost three hours' duration. The number of bags and particular substance determine the amount of time the session will last. Some sessions take longer to administer than others.

As the medications are flowing into your body, you may eat a snack or drink a beverage, listen to headphones, knit, read, or do anything in a passive mode. When the session is completed, the port is re-flushed, and a bandage cover is placed over it to minimize blood spotting on your garments. The bandage can be removed when you get home.

Overall, the chemo is a killing agent of the cancer cells. It will lower the white cell count in the patient's body, which is why the blood tests are performed weekly. Sometime during the chemo session you may receive a B12 shot to help boost the white cell count. The doctor explains the various ramifications, side-effects, and various stages of the chemo application. *No two people react the same way to any chemo session or time frame between chemo sessions.* Some folks lose hair; some don't. Some get nausea; others don't. It all depends on the individual physical and medical makeup of the person. Betty experienced minimal chemo discomfort. Luck, we guess.

What is the process of getting a radiation treatment? Not all cancer treatments involve radiation treatments, but if a chemo/radiation process is suggested, the two doctors will coordinate timing and dose amounts for the overall timeframe. On your initial visit to the radiation-oncologist location, he or she will explain the process in detail: which organ(s) will be targeted, how it will be treated, what, if any, side-effects are to be expected or may unexpectedly appear.

After the introduction to the process, the patient is taken back to the radiology room for radiation placement. You get a series of ink-marks on your body to be used in future radiation sessions. They are the laser alignment marks for specific focusing and registration of the radiation instrumentation. If you had a biopsy, the alignment markers placed in your body at the time of the biopsy assist your doctor in this planning phase. Again, this planning phase may take a little while. Once the planning session is completed, the actual radiation sessions will last about four to eight minutes per session (at least in our case for lung cancer). As I've said before, other cancer treatment sessions may last longer.

Whatever treatments you receive from the oncologist or radiation-oncologist, be sure to discuss all phases of your treatments, physical or emotional feelings, side-effects (loss of appetite, hair, skin rash), or anything out of the normal. These question sessions will be a great benefit to you and your doctor. Work with your advocate or friend. Maybe they see a change in you, which you don't realize is occurring in your overall makeup. It takes a team to make this journey—the more, the merrier!

The adjustment in the schedule was a major issue: Surgery was planned and executed between the second and third chemo treatments, and it had to be within a window suitable to the thoracic surgeon. This was a critical schedule adjustment. Originally, surgery was planned for the end of the chemo sessions. A layman's explanation is the lung has malleability (a condition seen in over-cleaning or tanning of leather hide). The lung had to be soft enough, but at the same time it could not be too soft —only determined by a surgeon's touch. The overall result in our case was that my wife lost two upper lobes of the right lung. The remaining lower third lobe on the right side filled 80 percent of the open space created by the loss of the two lobes. (As the advocate, your life's knowledge base of medical terminology and anatomy will be broadened by various explanations of the medical team members.)

The surgery was executed; recovery was sensitive and slow. The surgery was a serious procedure with an eight-day hospitalization period. The final result of the surgery was two major scars: a horizontal nine-inch scar and a silver dollar-size drain tube hole in the right side. See Pictures II and III.

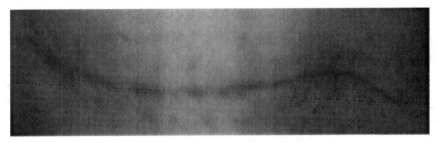

**Picture II – Side incision with staple marks –
Nine inches long, back to front**

**Picture III – Drain hole scar from tube inserted during surgery, about three
inches below side incision scar.**

Recovery from the surgery was slow and gradual. Nothing could be
rushed. Movements were slow and deliberate. Nothing should be
placed near the right side of the body. Walking was encouraged,
slowly at first; sitting up in a chair was a great effort. Eating was sparse
due to the loss of appetite, which was then regained over time
(weeks). Two months after the surgery, right-side movements were
still performed cautiously. Reaching for an object, such as a salt shaker
on the dinner table, was done slowly. Breathing required a respiratory
treatment with an inhaler at times, such as after going up the stairs
too quickly. Shortness of breath was an issue if walking too far. For
example, going from the kitchen to the mailbox (200 feet round trip)
might require sitting to rest and regain breathing tempo. Pain medication was prescribed and taken as needed, and eventually none was
needed. Time was the great healer from this surgical procedure. There

were no post-operative problems from the surgery. Slow progression to regain daily life activity takes TIME.

Chemo #3 did not occur until four weeks after the surgery. Chemo #3 was delivered, and we reestablished the isolation house lock-down. All was going well, until the day before Chemo #4 was to be delivered and monitored. She became markedly sick again. Having seen the pattern of illness—fever, vomiting, chills, etc.—we were back in the ER and checked for UTI immediately. The bug had returned, and at this writing a visit is planned with our urologist—soon! Why is she susceptible to UTIs and track problems? These issues will be determined later by the urologist.

The final Chemo #4 was delivered upon clearing the UTI problem, and all is well in the village. As with all cancer patients, some monitoring is in the lifecycle. A CT PET scan presented a normal result—no cancer cells in the body at this time.

In discovering and identifying the problem of cancer, bear in mind the constant realm of CHANGE. No two cancers with the same name are treated the same way, have the same problematic cancer cure process, or even use the same chemo cocktail ingredients. One lung cancer may opt for a preliminary first-level operation, while another cancer is treated by chemo and/or radiation first. More than likely, no two cancers of the same name are treated the same in the diagnosis, applicable treatments, and organ/tumor removal. The overall cancer process for treatment is determined by the collective team assembled for this patient. Too many factors are relevant to the decision, timing, and execution of the process and plan. Ask questions, listen, and learn of your problem and solution.

These questions have a direct target to a lung cancer patient. Most of them are applicable to other types of cancer patients as well, however.

Different docs will likely respond with other answers…choose wisely.

Most of these questions should be answered by your oncologist and/or radiation-oncologist. Just as you would like these questions answered, each doctor and medical person will also be asking you applicable questions.

As the author of *The Journey,* I can easily present the answers to all the questions, but the answer will have a greater impact when you read the question and write the answer based on the doctor's reply—*and* hear the answer from your doctor.

The questions are presented in a matrix so you may enter your answers more easily. Keep in mind the goal—you must have a goal—to be cancer-free.

Question	Answer
How was the cancer discovered? From an examination? X-ray/scan? You felt poorly and went to the doctor?	
Was a biopsy performed? Invasive or through the esophagus?	
Are the lymph nodes directly involved?	
Has the stage of the biopsy results been determined?	
Has the stage been re-assessed by an independent party and con- firmed equal to the biopsy analysis laboratory?	

Question	Answer
Have the stage results been explained to you? HOW are the stage results determined? Recall the National Cancer Institute is available to you for overall cancer assistance. How can you use them, or should you use their services?	
What is the game plan?	
What comes first and why? • Chemo • Surgery • Radiation	
What is the time frame between each application or session, and why?	
Will I need a B12 shot each week?	
Will my white blood cell counts be taken and evaluated each week while on chemo? How? Where?	
If the white cell counts are exceptionally low, what is the immediate procedure?	
Am I required to be home-bound (isolated) during the chemo time frame? Explain (minimizing all contact with humanity reduces the possibility of ingesting airborne diseases [flu, coughs, sneezes] thereby affecting the white blood count).	

Question	Answer
Describe the time line of the side-effects of each procedure? (Chemo and radiation have distinct times/side-effects by days after receiving the application.)	
What medication can be taken to minimize the procedure's side-effects? An over-the-counter med-ication will minimize the side-effects of chemo. This medica-tion, which reduces agitation in the stomach, is recommended to be taken daily, even before chemo begins.	
When and where will a chest port be installed in your shoulder area, and by whom?	
What is a port? And why should you have one in this procedure?	
What is the full cycle of each chemo? (Chemo application varies by the types of medications sug-gested by the oncologist.) Have each described, targeted use, expected results, measured by ___, and the side-effects (medically, nausea, hair loss, red welts on the skin, others?).	
How many bags are included in a chemo application? Drip time duration? Food recommendations?	

Question	Answer
Where do you have to travel to receive the chemo application?	
Describe chemo and what it does. Will I feel any immediate affects inside or on my body?	
What are the radiologist/oncologist prep procedures? Template measurements, clothes restrictions, or removal?	
What is the goal of the radiation application? Reduce the tumor? Eliminate the tumor? Both? Explain the side-effects of this procedure.	
What medications or external creams can be applied to reduce skin irritation?	
What is my financial responsibility for this therapy from each doctor? Provide them your insurance carrier information, and upon your next visit, the doctor (or his office manager) should be able to detail your potential cost. Additional discussion may be needed with the doctor.	
Given any situation during the therapy time, who do I call when an abnormality occurs? Phone and time? Example: Four days after a chemo application, you come down with a 102-degree fever, are vomiting, and feeling achy all over. Call XYZ. Do this NOW. Follow the directions, maybe go to the hospital ER for ???	

Question	Answer
Do I need a caregiver support person? Advocate? An additional sounding board to reaffirm medical discussions, etc.? Bear in mind earlier discussions recommending you do not go through the cancer rehabilitation process alone. You may need additional assistance at your home—cleaning folks, people to assist in food preparation, or folks who help with driving you to/from doctors' appointments or other activities.	

Keep your friends informed…. I used the UPDATES

CHAPTER 6

The Updates

This chapter of *The Journey* includes the status reports of my wife's condition as she passed various stages. Mention is made to the evolution of *change,* as presented earlier, and the different stages. CHANGE HAPPENS. Expect it, accept it, go with it, and be ready for the next level of change.

Initially, the updates were sent to a small group of friends and associates. By the time Update 5 came out, it had become a small e-mail blast to more than a hundred people. My wife's condition was of great concern to all. There are nine update messages in all. I've included the updates to guide you through a similar format or style if you care to replicate an update to your friends and acquaintances. I have include a brief comment for you after each update message. Your call. I present:

Update #1

Greetings,

As of today, there are 4 radiation sessions remaining – completing next Tuesday. Rad session is a 45 gray blast – about 4 - 7 minutes.

There are 2 Chemo sessions (10/15, 11/5) left. 5 bags, 2 anti-nausea, 1 steroid, 1 Alimta, 1 carboplaten

Nov 18th a PET scan will be done to assess over rad / chemo applications.

First week in Dec (date TBD) – surgery will be done to remove the mass, a portion of the lung, and the affected lymph node. Hospital stay 5 to 7 days at old Holy Cross Hospital.

Cancer free – monitoring planned.

Only had one bad nausea evening…. Otherwise mid-day naps are usually the case. Eating ok, probably won't lose her hair – bought an expensive wig!!

Progressing – day by day.

Have a great trip…. Thanks for the support.

Regards,

Jim

"Standing by, waiting, and ok – a few naps are planned." This message came from a naïve guardian (ME) who was not ready to be a watchman at the time. You must learn early on to be vigilant and ready for the next challenge. It will come when you least expect it.

Update #2

Greets folks,

*Got bad news in Mudville today..... Betty has been hospital-
ized since Monday night with a 103+ fever. It broke Wed
AM.... Why the fever? A UTI. Sound familiar? Yep, says the
Drs (Plural).... She needs antibiotics and let her go home.... I
wouldn't take that answer and wanted more information –
Hey, I said: she hasn't had a CT Scan of the lower GI since all
this mess started – the catch phrase of the DRs... we'll review
the charts!! (Remember in June it was a UTI that had the
same symptoms and the ER doc said let's take a chest x-ray to
see if you're OK)... OK hell – there's something in your lung
area....get your regular doc to check it out..... THE MASS was
found and you know the rest there.*

*Review my ass.... There weren't any charts so the lower CT scan
was ordered and low and behold.... Another (forgot the term)
was found on the left kidney.... Not cancerous, but definitely the
cause of the UTI problems.... I actually got an ATTA BOY NICE
THINKING from the DR!!!! I thanked him for hearing me.*

*They brought in our urology doc, more tests today - but confi-
dent this cyst will dissipate with lots of antibiotics, and Chemo
will resume in about 2 weeks. All this happened just one day
BEFORE the 3rd chemo dose..... lucky break there. The main
schedule has been slipped 2 weeks for fever recovery.... Okay it
slips – overall feeling is better today since Monday. Should be
home this weekend, probably NLT Monday.*

*The cancer doc said this was routine, and he expected a fever
blast but not this close to the 3rd chemo.... He didn't expect to
find or know about a kidney problem. They were going to treat
it as a chemo reaction. Glad that changed.*

All in all – Betty is doing better than expected with going thru 25 radiation blasts and the 2 chemos to-date. NOW THE GOOD NEWS..... Got to have take away moment and smile!!!!! As a result of the tests taken this week to figure out the high fever..... X-rays show the lung mass has been reduced in size. For this revelation to be seen on an X-RAY is significant due to the fact the x-ray doesn't normally show mass sizes. This is attributed to the 2 chemos and 25 rad treatments.... Yea team....

It also means the lymph should have been reduced also!!

Keep the prayers coming.... Like I said – God is multi-lingual, English, Chinese, Japanese, and Korean – that's funny – we embroider in all those languages!!!! To Happy in China, T – Japanese, and T in Hungul, Eric's denominational church... .... Keep joining our American friends..... I'm sure the prayers are working.

The dogs and I are doing fine – with help from our neighbor and the understanding and prayers from our St. Paul Community (Fr. Joe, pass it around please), Post 171 – Sam pass around please) .... Thank you all.

Jim

Update #2 began the process of being more inclusive of information to the group. It explained the UTI and the delay impact on the overall healing schedule. Flexibility is a key factor in dealing with the medical world AND keeping a sane head for yourself. The journey continues.

Update #3

Dear friends,

Status report #3 – change happens, anticipate change, monitor change, and adapt to change quickly, change, enjoy change, and be ready to quickly change again and again. In the world of cancer patients – change happens – sometimes quickly, slowly, with great impact or minor occurrences. Betty has had several changes since the last update.

To make an exhaustive story short... as I mentioned before – the primary tumor has reduced in size. I am told there is a significant reduction in the size of the mass in the upper lung. The lymph node has also reduced in size..... yea team.... Radiation worked with 2 bouts of chemo. Again, more change – due to the UTI problem, it threw off the original schedule, so now surgery to remove the mass and lung (or portion thereof), and the lymph will be on Nov 17 – 11 AM. The Dr has told me she will be in the hospital 7 to 10 days – I expect change!! Upon a rest and healing time frame – TBD, she will receive the last 2 chemo sessions. Chemo is administered 3 weeks apart - 5 bags of STUFF over a 2.5 hour time frame. Betty really does handle the chemo well – very little side effects.

We have plans for neighbor support for the animals. We are preparing for change when Betty gets home. I expect a slow to modest recovery from this type of surgery. Our house is 100 feet long.... I do not expect any 100 feet dashes in the first week home. BUT – walking movement is greatly encouraged. She'll get up for food or money.... And since she's not spending or making any money while she's resting.... She'll come to the kitchen for food!! Yea – I can bring snacks to the bedroom and a few dog treats too – got to feed all the animals in this house!!!

E-Z Stitches is in a modest hold for the time being. We are clearing out current orders and telling customers there will be a slight delay in filling your Dec. order. Most understand – emergency orders will get filled by me or Vince. The show will go on.... More change.

The April carrot is very much in the works..... After all this cancer crap, Betty and I will be spending our 37th anniversary on the island of St. Lucia in the Caribbean.... The goal is eminent. Have to buy sandals and a few t-shirts when I'm there. Come on April!!!! We will enjoy this change.

Again, keep the prayers going NORTH to our God... I know He has heard all of us – the changes are of His doing – and only He knows the reason for these movements. We are pawns in this chess game subject to the Master's Mind.

My subscription to life is – Everything happens for a reason – and sometimes the reason is not immediately obvious... but for a reason. So – prayers are needed in earnest to help Betty and me get thru this roadblock in life's path. We are all better thru prayer. God changes all of us. Thank you all.

Sincerely,

Jim

The UTI issue has created its own level of chaos. It is the initiator for several quick change activities, meds to take, necessary meals to create, or open a can of soup. Got a little testy during this update... this too shall pass, and it did.

A life lesson

In dealing with the myriad of doctors, lab tests, and blocks of time waiting for the next decision or action event, there were lots of moments to think—think about our lives (together 37 years), about the variety of previous medical challenges for both of us, the birth of our son, our happier moments of vacations and visiting antique stores—and your mind rambles. Cancer is rotten, and it can take over your mind and thoughts. Patience was needed to stay focused on the goal: my healthy mate. The following story puts life into a positive perspective of winning the time game.

The Story of a Thousand Marbles

A few weeks ago, I was shuffling off to my ham radio shack with a steaming cup of coffee in one hand and the morning paper in the other. What began as a typical Saturday morning turned into one of those lessons life seems to hand you from time to time. Let me tell you about it.

I turned up the radio volume and heard a golden baritone voice from an older gentleman. You know the kind—he sounded like he should be in the broadcasting business. I was intrigued and stopped to listen to what he had to say.

"Well, Tom, it sure sounds like you're busy with your job. I'm sure they pay you well, but it's a shame you have to be away from home and your family so much. Hard to believe a young fellow should have to work sixty or seventy hours a week to make ends meet. Too bad you missed your daughter's dance recital."

He continued, "Let me tell you something, Tom, something that has helped me keep a good perspective on my own priorities." And that's when he began to explain his theory of a thousand marbles. "You see, I sat down one day and did a little arithmetic. The average person lives about seventy-five years. I know some live more, and some live less, but on average, folks live about seventy-five years."

"Now then, I multiplied seventy-five times fifty-two and I came up with thirty-nine hundred, which is the number of Saturdays that the average person has in their entire lifetime. Now stick with me, Tom. I'm getting to the important part."

"It took me until I was fifty-five years old to think about all this in any detail," he went on. "And by that time I had lived through over twenty-eight hundred Saturdays. I got to thinking that if I lived to be seventy-five, I only had about a thousand Saturdays left to enjoy."

"So I went to a toy store and bought every single marble they had. I ended up having to visit three toy stores to round-up one thousand marbles. I took them home and put them inside of a large, clear plastic container right here in the shack next to my gear. Every Saturday since then, I have taken one marble out and thrown it away."

"I found that by watching the marbles diminish, I focused more on the really important things in life. There is nothing like watching your time here on this earth run out to help get your priorities straight."

"Now let me tell you one last thing before I sign-off with you and take my lovely wife out for breakfast. This morning, I took the very last marble out of the container. I figure if I make it until next Saturday then I have been given a little extra time. And the one thing we can all use is a little more time."

"It was nice to meet you, Tom. I hope you spend more time with your family, and I hope to meet you again."

You could have heard a pin drop on the radio when this fellow signed off. I guess he gave us all a lot to think about. I had planned to work that morning. Instead, I went upstairs and woke my wife up with a kiss. "C'mon honey, I'm taking you and the kids to breakfast."

"What brought this on?" she asked with a smile.

"Oh, nothing special. It's just been a while since we spent a Saturday together with the kids. Hey, can we stop at a toy store while we're out? I need to buy some marbles."

Source: Anonymous – received by e-mail in mid-nineties.

Update #4

Greets folks,

And recall the last update – "Adapt to Change quickly" – wow what a change occurred yesterday. We were told to report to the hospital at 9AM for an additional breathing test. We did, neat test, illustrates lung breathing capacity at various levels.

Surgery for the lung/lymph was scheduled for 1PM. Due to a Barnum & Bailey environment in the operation room we had a 5.5 hour delay to begin the surgery. Betty went into surgery at 6:30PM, the surgery lasted 3.5 hours. I met with the Dr at 10:15 PM... bottom line – Betty did fantastic and all expected results were met. Without going into explicit details of bits and pieces, she will remain in the PACU/ICU for a couple of days before going to a recovery room.

The Dr told me about future expected progress. Let's just say, Betty will not be allowed to paint the house or vacuum right handed for a couple of days. I saw Betty in the PACU; she was asleep and wired up for her comfort. I got home at midnight.

My neighbor has assisted with Shadow & Brandi, our two res- cued border collies/ Labradors – they wanted to play for 45 minutes, glad to see me. Got to bed at 1:15AM and up at 5:30 with Brandi's barks to go out... they tell you when they have to go out.... And you must listen and obey – Who trains who??

I will be departing for the hospital 10ish, got some work to do here at the house, like this update and mail review.

I cannot say thank you enough for all the prayers and good intentions for Betty – everything paid off the right way. Lessons learned will not be apparently shown, but we all talked to God in unison and devotion. Thank you thank you... Please continue the heavenly chatter – we're not totally out of the woods yet – recovery will be slow for the next few weeks. We have adapted to change quickly, and will be ready to change quickly back to normal life...haha around here – WHAT's Normal??

This morning in MD – it is 8 degrees at 6:30 AM COLD.... No snow yet, none expected so far.

All the best folks, and thanks again.

Jim

As referenced earlier in the Team chapter, you cannot go through the cancer parade alone! You need supporting players in your corner to assist in the full process. Cancer survivors are tigers waiting for the next event. And the event must include other participants.

Update #5

Greetings All,

Some of you are new to the update list so a little refresher is in order. Update 3# said.... change happens, anticipate change, monitor change, adapt to change quickly, change, enjoy change, and be ready to quickly change again and again. In the world of cancer patients – change happens – sometimes quickly, slowly, with great impact or minor occurrences. Betty has had several changes since the last update.

I must now inform you of the changes since updates #3 & #4 – yes change happened but this time slowly AND quickly – and for the good. What is the proverb, "Make haste – slowly".

Last Monday was a terribly long day for Betty and I – we arrived at the hospital at the designated time 9AM for a pulmonary test before the operation at 1PM.... 1, 2, 3, 4, 5 PMs later.... She was taken into the operating room at 6:30PM – 10PM, I was informed "a little while longer – everything is going well", 10:30PM, I meet with the DR, we chat for 30 minutes – all went well and he took me back to see Betty. She was asleep –with lots of tubes and monitors around the bed. The cancerous tumor and related lymph nodes were removed along with 2 lung lobes on the right side. (FYI – the remaining lobe on the right side will expand over time and fill the open cavity.) I got home at midnight. The dogs were happy to see me. (Thanks to the Huguleys for many hours of dog watching, outside play and lots of prayers). Prayers – another issue!!!

Every day I would go to the hospital, taking the AM- PM shift, and Vince would take the PM night shift after his work (archi-

tect in Baltimore) and we would watch the transformation of a very passive patient in CCU into a person capable of sitting up 3 hours in a different unit with 7 tubes in place!!! CHANGE happens … s l o w l y…. Saturday a couple of tubes came out…. Sunday, the rest came out and MONDAY TODAY….. Betty is coming out – home!!!!! Yea team…… it is 6 AM as I write this – dogs have been fed and out, emails read, and this is being composed for you. I'm awaiting the call…. "Come get me".

Saturday afternoon, 3:30PM we met with the DR and his criteria for release before Thanksgiving were medical milestones. She met them, one after the other between Saturday/Sunday, i.e. 4 clean chest x-rays, vertical movement, and walking time – among others. Sunday – she finished the list and was told Monday you could go home. WOW… The person I saw Monday at 11PM is not the same person I saw yesterday at 2PM…. All in all, we have some follow-up visits to the DRs, remove staples, x-rays, and schedule 2 more chemos – piece of cake compared to the last 4 months. Ya know – sometimes it is hard to type with tears in your eyes… tried to catch the typos.

So – as for Change happens, and embrace change…. We're doing it – all thru the prayers of many of you, and folks we haven't met to say thank you. God listened to all of us – all because I spread the word and asked for and got help and volunteered action of "We'll pray for you and her". Even the DR asked me, "How was I doing" (couple of days I looked a little dragged – I'm sure) – getting thru – one day at a time.

Without you this email would not be possible and as positive an outcome – so from the bottom of our hearts – thank you over and over again.

We are not out of the woods by any means, but we're a sure lot closer to returning to human life prior to the cancer diagnosis. We're getting there – with change – slowly.

We are adopting to change, and expecting more changes ...
The goal is now in sight – St. Lucia – last week of April 2015
– 37th wedding anniversary – we'll be there – cheers!

Jim

This update expresses the frustration of the waiting event. Cancer is brutal and keeps beating on you. *The Journey* presents the efforts and resolves to monitor and change a lung cancer patient. Each cancer is different, unique, and returns unexpected results from what should be routine tests. As the guardian and advocate, the watchwords today are "stay focused." The goal and prize is in sight —recovery!

Update #6

Greetings All,

In life the reality of the CHANGE PROCESS is a necessity for a peaceful mind and life cycle. This last week included more changes.

Yep – we were cleared to go home Monday..... Did not leave the hospital until 6PM – a paper work snafu – patience... the hospital has lots of patience.... I DON"T!!!!! But – we got cleared and out of there – to head home. En-route we planned on stopping at the local Damascus CVS pharmacy to get 2 RXs filled – the CVS pharmacy has no power (EAST COAST OUTAGE for all CVS stores) to bill the scripts – went to the SAFEWAY and the lady did magic to get us the meds – without an insurance card!!!! Love ya Vera!!! Got home at 8:10PM and the week begins to the phrase of another favorite columnist – Linda Elerby – "And So It Goes"....

The hospital follow-up folks called today to check on Betty (now asleep) and wanted to know why we refused a home health care RN? I said "We refused nothing, we were not offered the opportunity to obtain a home health care RN – and THAT started the issue that stopped at the Hospital Administrator – one of his staff screwed up – big time!!!! Now resolved – expecting a scheduling call soon. (Goes back to an earlier update note – You don't want to see this BULL coming to YOUR glass antique shop!!!) (Did I say that politely and with conviction?) Anyway – we'll have home health care attention.

After discussion with the DR office, the RXs have to be taken every 3 hours, so one of the meds obtained Monday night had to be changed – too much Tylenol (it affects the liver, and chemo affects the liver too – had to reduce the Tylenol content) so the new script cannot be faxed or called in – you have to go to the DR office and pickup the RX and take it to the pharmacy – with 2 forms of ID – this is not a joke…. So now it's Wednesday and we are expecting 2-4 inches of snow beginning at 10AM…. (Finishing the update Friday AM)…. We got 3 slushy inches – enough to clean & wipe the dog's feet each time they go out and come inside.

Betty is spending most of the days sleeping/resting and taking her meds. Thanksgiving Day, Vince and Stephanie brought over a complete Thanksgiving Day meal for the four of us. WOW – Betty came to the dining room, ate and visited with them – Steph graduates law school in May 2015 – always busy cramming for exams. This gift came complete with cleanup!!!! Great idea – we loved it.

With all the cancer prep meetings – no one, not one single DR or support person mentioned the rehab time and effort. It is extensively slow and sometimes – even with meds – painful. This CHANGE process is not for the fast pace movers…. Progress (change) is slow and noticeable…. You feel better and there is less pain – one step forward – sometimes a couple of steps back – not always – that is good!!! We embrace it, because more change is coming in the healing process. Cancer in any form is ruthless and, at times – the cure is worse than the disease. Don't lose sight of the prize – the quality of life improves with time. Visiting NFL Coaches probably tell their teams, "We're not here to lose". And so we are here for the game and the victory… press on my friends.

Don't stop your prayers…. We make progress because God listens to each of us. He knows how much Betty is cared for by so *many people and groups of folks... She is an important lad, to each of us.*

And God also provides comedy.... After the Monday ordeal and Tuesday long rest time, a good friend sent an email offering to bring us dinner that evening – I read the email at 6AM and replied, "that would be nice – thanks". At about 2PM, Betty asked me what I was making for dinner – so I picked up the phone and called our friend – and asked for "ROOM SER-VICE???" – We all laughed – what is for dinner and when will it be brought to the room? She delivered a delicious chicken pot pie, including dessert and sides.... Thanks JB. There are great moments to cherish and smile about.

Lessons learned.... Don't lose your sense of humor and stay focused on the prize – a new day, on the top of the dirt, smelling the roses, and helping others. Even being a little (or a lot) under the weather in recovery – we help others, who offer to help us. It is a circle and the prize is only known to the inner self. I'm sure you understand about feeling good inside – "Put some money in the Salvation Army kettle" – you should have a smile on your face.

"Be ready to quickly change again and again..." and my last life lesson for the day.... "I do not worry about anything I don't control" God is in control of everything... go with it, and be ready to change quickly .....

Thank you all for prayers, calls, encouragement, and friendship... we're getting there – wherever there is... one day at a time.

Jim

The patient must be able fend for himself or herself—cook, wash, and clean. Progress slowly and remember the tide will change one day—quickly and unannounced. The marriage bond and commitment helps reinforce why we do what we do—because we do.

Update #7

Greetings team,

There is joy in Mudville today >>>> all 23 staples were removed and we were told the remaining lung lobe (on the right side) has inflated correctly and is very functional.

The internal healing will continue for some time, but the overall prognosis is great. PT and OT have begun coming to help coordinate some exercises for upper body strength. They are pleased with the outcome of the surgery also.

The weather in the MD area has been hot, cold, colder, and rainy the last few days. It will be some time before Betty regains herself, prior to last June. BUT she is here to recover nicely from this ordeal.

The remaining 2 chemos are still pending – restart date TBD next week – since she didn't have difficulty with the first 2 – we see no problem with the last two sessions. The next surgeon's appt / CT PET scan is set for March 2015.

Prayers in the God–cancer bucket have overflowed for Betty – and we greatly appreciate all of them. We need to find a cure for these ugly diseases – so don't stop the prayer lines.

After the PET Scan, we're packing for April, and sun, beaches, and no stress!!!

All the best to each of you, and thank you, thank you, and thank you….

Jim

Not all updates are lengthy…. Some are just short notes. She was feeling better and coming along nicely. Two more updates…then she does the cooking!

Update #8

Good morning folks, and welcome to UPDATE#8. Since our last report, Betty has been trying to improve with the help of OT and PT visits as ordered by our Dr. There has been some improvement. But no major leaping strides of success.

We were at the DR (oncologist) office yesterday for a status update, and as of now chemo will NOT start just yet. Betty's appetite has not increased, still losing weight, pain has not been greatly reduced (still on pain meds) and her general status is not 100% perky. The scar from the operation shows no problems with infection or leakage. It is the muscle healing under the scar that is the pain problem. To be expected due to the size and complexity of the operation. Overall status – on track, so we'll wait a bit on the last 2 chemos.

Keep in mind - monitor change – that is exactly what we are doing…. Because we will adapt to change and be ready to change again as needed. Betty is cancer-free – and the cure is worse than the disease – but necessary. Keep in mind not all cancer problems are over in six months. We have been blessed and do count our blessings.

Based upon some new prescriptions, and next week's blood work and DR visit, we'll have a better handle on the next chemo date – probably the first week in January. These last 2 chemos are important – they will "clean up" any residual lingering cancer cells from the initial onset of the lung cancer.

Keep your prayers flooding the market for not just Betty, but for all cancer patients, young and old. Remember when breast cancer was a death sentence? All cancer can and will be beaten in time. You might have a lasting scar or side effect –

BUT you're on the top side of the dirt to show off your markings and your smiles!!!

The OLD fashion gall bladder operation left a 12 inches long scar across the patient's abdomen – the new procedure approved by the FDA now leaves 3 one inch incisions to remove the gall bladder. Oh well…. More change for the better.

To all of you who have sent cards, and calls, and "Tell Betty…" we thank you, and keep thanking you for all your support. As I have said… you need a strong support team to beat this problem – and you are members of our team. AGAIN Many thanks.

Merry Christmas to all and have a prosperous and healthy New Year…. 2015 – gonna be a great year for everyone.

Back to ya then… The DR is in…. take 2 aspirin and call me in the AM – five cents please!!

Jim

This update was one coming close to the end of the line for information flow. Actually, update #9 was the last one published to the group. YOU ARE ALL TEAM MEMBERS…. That is the take away message for this complete process. The journey, roadblocks, ditches, and problems are made easier when a teammate is there to comfort you and help you through the issue at hand.

Update #9

Update # 9 – the closing chapter. Coming from Chicago, and attending many many Chicago Cubs baseball games, when Ernie Banks (who just recently passed away last week at 83), hit a home run, the announcer, Jack Brickhouse – would expound with "HEY HEY" (also picked up Harry Carry). Well folks…. It's HEY HEY time here. Betty is cancer free – amen!

There is no simple way to express our gratitude for all the support, prayers, levels of assistance, and overall well wishes from countless friends, associates and even strangers. To all of you who have sent cards, and calls, and "Tell Betty…" we thank you, and keep thanking you for all your support. As I have said… you need a strong support team to beat cancer – and you are members of our team. AGAIN Many thanks.

"HEY HEY….HEE HEE strange things are happening"…. Quotiff the comic – Red Buttons…. Chemo is a brutal poison destroying the cancer cells, and at times, affects other parts of the body with potential infection, and LOWERS the white cell count. Chemo is supposed to cause hair loss. Betty's hair is intact, showing a little more gray, but not too much in density loss. (Probably because we bought an expensive wig – never worn – ok by me – I don't have much hair anyway!)

The surgery in November removed the cancer mass and 2 parts of the right lung. The third part of the right lung (called the lower lob) has filled the lung cavity quicker than expected. She has good capacity in both lungs.

Tomorrow is the final chemo session, and with minimal side effects (as has been the case with the previous 3 chemo sessions), Chemo 3 & 4 are the chemo to clean out the blood system, and any organs that may have potential cancer cells floating in the body. February 21ˢᵗ will be declared.... No more cancer cell or treatments. We still have to be monitored in the future months – as do all cancer patients for a period of time (ours is TBD). But – in a declaration of enthusiasm.... IT IS OVER!

Change Happens – in time – it sure does, Anticipate Change – we are currently buying clothes for the April trip, Monitor Change – you bet we are, Adapt to change quickly – no faster than we can leave the DR's office – yep, CHANGE – with prayer and patients – we have, Enjoy Change – after 2/21 – we surely will, and finally – Be ready to quickly change again and again, a needed observation and constant attendance in life's lesson.

Keep your prayers flooding the market for not just Betty, but for all cancer patients, young and old. Remember when breast cancer was a death sentence? All cancer can and will be beaten in time. You might have a lasting scar or side effect – BUT you're on the top side of the dirt to show off your markings and your smiles!!!

The DR is OUT for the time being – keep your five cents please!! All the best to all of you.... It's been a long road but IT"S OVER!!! Thank you

Jim

And the 100 bottles of beers came off the wall, and the song was over... *if one of those bottles should happen to fall, zero bottles of beer on the wall.* The journey does not end here. We're at a rest stop, not sure of the ultimate destination or road to take to get somewhere. We'll resume the everyday living, but a little more slowly. (Things will get done, and friends will share in the glad times we are well and smiling.) And so life goes on, and we beat this devil this time...until the next challenge, my friend.

There is always more sand in the bottle.

CHAPTER 7

The Conclusion, Not the End

The goal was to be cancer-free. We have met the goal—at a price. Time has to be paid to the keeper, for the last two chemo treatements were extensive and drawn out due to the additional UTI problems. The recovery time has been extended to an unknown date. Actually, some days are reasonably OK, but then some days are a killer and the right underarm chest pain is prolonged for the day. More Tylenol or prescribed pain medication is taken as needed. A chest operation requires several muscles to be sliced to provide space to remove a lung mass and lobe; ribs must be separated for space and access. The body must heal and recover from this procedure in due time.

As the "end" draws near, when do you know it is the end? Still pending are two more scans and a few doctor visits to officially be cleared as a cancer-free patient having gone through the last seven months of the process, the procedures, and the recovery. In the months to come, there will be periodic testing to ensure the body system is stable, the white blood count is within range, and the overall body systems do not show signs of cancer cell accumulation.

Physical repair will be done in *time*. The body will recuperate at its own pace with proper food nutrition of proteins, and vitamins. In the last 8 months, Betty lost twenty-five pounds without exercise. Time to regain some of the body structure and readjust clothes sizes. This diet is not recommended for the average dieter.

The carrot for going through the journey is a trip to the Caribbean island of St. Lucia. As we began the journey through the cure of cancer, I wanted a stress-reliever for both of us—an over-all pleasure spot to rest and not be concerned about customer requests, documentation, or system reviews—so (having been to the Caribbean several times) I chose St. Lucia. Our honeymoon resort on Barbados has been destroyed, so we opted out of the memorable location. The carrot is close, and the patient is recovering slowly. We will make the trip! Happy 37th anniversary!!

Can you see the future?

CHAPTER 8

What's Coming?

Anoted cancer oncologist and acquaintance provided this observation. At the time of this discussion, Betty was about to complete six months through the Lung Cancer Journey, and he spoke to me.

Keep in mind the original cancer mass—a substantial mass the size of a golf ball—has made a dramatic entrance into my wife's body. It came with no announcement or symptoms. It has had time to circulate throughout the entire body and visit other organs. The cancer is in the blood stream and now circulates freely. Using the approach taken by Dr. (the oncologist) and Dr. (the radiologist/oncologist), we attack the mass through chemotherapy AND radiology. The two chemo treatments and twenty-five radiation sessions were aggressive maneuvers to reduce the lung mass cancer and possibly minimize the cancer transfer to other organs, such as the liver or pancreas. The biopsies indicated lymph nodes were affected by the lung cancer mass.

The process identified early-on is the correct approach to this type of lung cancer and for this stage at diagnosis, even considering the interruption in the cure process by the UTIs. Ultimately, the process includes a surgical removal of the lung/lymph mass organs. A final CT PET scan indicated a successful treatment to remove the cancer from the lung cavity.

Bear in mind the previous paragraph. Cancer has entered the body and will now be silent for a period of time. The third and fourth chemo treatments are called "cleanup chemos," and they are meant to ultimately drive out and kill the residual cancer cells in the blood system. Therein is the definition of the term "long-term cancer-free."

A lung cancer-free patient YEARS in remission is a successful cancer-free patient. Lung cancer patients who are coming out of surgical treatment are, in fact, cancer-free, but need to be conscious of the sleeping cells in the body. The long-term cells will "nap" anywhere from three to five years and may appear in some other organ. Or they may continue to nap through the five-year stretch into the seven-year window. Remaining in remission past the seven-year mark is a successful indication the patient is, in fact, cancer-free.

Percentage statistics are available for these levels of case analysis, but they demonstrate a case percentage of activity for the overall lung cancer population. Each cancer patient may or may not directly relate to the survey due to numerous treatment variables and conditions (i.e., does the multiple-UTI factor affect the patient cancer cell generation or reduction?). Other parameters must be considered.

Cancer patients must regularly take a CT PET scan for the monitoring of the sleeping cancer cells within the body. At the moment, this is the easiest and earliest detection of cancer movement, re-activation, or regeneration in other body organs. Clean results are most eagerly anticipated and reported to the patient. Results of potential organ challenges are also relayed but with a discussion of possible treatment of an infected area or organ.

Patients who are cancer-free smile and are glad to see another day. For it is in the realization you have beaten the devil at his own game—and won! Congratulations!

CHAPTER 9

Monumental

On October 19, 2015, after fifteen months of diagnosed lung cancer, the last of the process to be executed was the removal of the chemo port from my wife's left shoulder. As with each surgical procedure, the doctor and I met before and after the operation. We discussed what was to be done, amount of time in the OR, supporting staff of doctors and nurses, and the outcome results. It was during the last meeting our doc used the phrase, "This case was monumental in several ways." We had some small talk and then departed. Upon exiting the hospital, my wife wanted something to eat and a cup of coffee. It was during the coffee break that I brought up what the doc had said about being monumental. We thought about the last fifteen months and the reality of what we had been through. Collectively, by following the process—the process was the monumental accomplishment. Following are the steps of the process:

- Going to the ER for a severe upset stomach, diagnosed as a UTI, and getting a chest x-ray as a precaution, with the results of said x-ray being told, "Go see your regular doc. You have a spot on the x-ray."
- Our doc wanted a CT-scan.
- Referred to a surgeon.
- Met with the surgeon. We didn't like him, so we fired him. Follow your feelings about your docs—it is very important. You're going to be with him (or her or them) a long while through this process.
- Met with another surgeon—great doctor, good relations, and detailed explanations. He orders a CT PET scan. More details of the golf ball-size mass diagnosed in the lung.

- A biopsy is ordered, also referred to a pulmonary specialist. Lymph nodes are anticipated in the mass observation.
- Two biopsies are performed in the operating room using new technology through the esophagus and into the lung and through the esophagus to reach the lymph nodes. Interesting procedure called *bronchoscopy*.
- The biopsy slides were also analyzed by the National Cancer Institute in Bethesda, Maryland.
- After six weeks, we have a confirmed diagnosis of lung cancer Stage 3A by both analysis laboratories (Holy Cross Hospital and National Cancer Institute).
- With a confirmed diagnosis, we now have a path for resolution. At this stage, resolution is unknown, except we know we're off to see more docs.
- After conferring with our primary doctor and the surgeon, we agree on an oncologist relatively close to our home.
- The meeting lasted more than an hour with the oncologist. He answered all the questions we had, laid out the treatment, named the drugs to be used and any side-effects, and referred us to an associate oncologist/radiologist for radiation therapy at the same time as the chemo applications.
- After this meeting, it was determined a chemo port should be installed for the ease of the infusion of the chemo drugs.
- Back to the surgeon for the installation of a chemo port—left shoulder.
- We met with the radiation oncologist who also explained every step of the process in detail, including the definition of the term "Stage 3A," with visual graphics provided by biopsy images. I can't explain it here, but there is a formula to determine what level and cancer stage is being treated. Very interesting and informative.
- Our treatment included four applications of chemo, three weeks apart, and an immediate application of radiation for

twenty-five consecutive sessions (Monday through Friday with weekends off for the next five weeks).

- Following all prescribed doses of medication/radiation, surgery will be scheduled to remove the cancer growth and/or the lung, in total or designated lobe(s).
- We followed the process until another eruption of a UTI had to be treated and delayed the projected schedule by three weeks. Additional testing had to be scheduled to determine the cause of the UTI. A kidney infection required additional medication before chemo could be resumed—another delay based upon the urologist application of the meds.
- Two applications of chemo were administered, and the UTI delay caused the schedule to be adjusted, and surgery had to be scheduled as soon as the urologist approved the timing for the surgery.
- The surgery lasted almost four hours. During the surgery, it was determined two lobes of the right lung had to be removed along with a number of lymph nodes. Hospitalization time: nine days. Steady improvement during the next four weeks.
- After the lung was removed, two more chemo sessions were required to "clean up" any lingering residual cancer cells in the body.
- We followed the process identified nine months earlier, and it worked. All participants were fully involved, and their staff members equally supportive and caring.
- After the removal of the chemo port, all participants can echo the theme of the surgeon…"This was a monumental case." Thank you, Dr. S.

We Are Survivors

CHAPTER 10

The Survivors

This was the last chapter of *The Journey* to be written. It was also the most difficult to write because it encompasses two distinct types of survivorship: the cancer-free individual, or the person in remission, and the family members or friends of the deceased cancer victim. Each survivor has his or her unique story or levels of strain, pain, and anguish needed to recover from the event. Such an event could cause a few weeks or many months or even years of turmoil and unrest in battling the demon and disease.

The person in remission has gone through the journey and the ordeal of the cancer process to be declared cancer-free/in remission. As described earlier, routine tests and observations will still need to be taken periodically and analyzed. The "sleeping giant" could awaken at any unknown time in life's progress—a different organ or location or combination of instances or symptoms all to be monitored for the "just in case" unknown spot on a scan or X-ray. At times, it is the proverbial swinging pendulum, which may or may not have an automatic decreasing lowering momentum motion. Time is this person's advocate, adversary, and status quo. Prayer and observations are the lifeline for friends and the individual. Again, you cannot survive this alone.

The loss of life due to cancer is a terrible situation. This loss affects not only the patient but also the survivors—the spouse, children, siblings, friends, and associates. The death is real, the loss is real, and, depending on the length of the degrading life span (i.e. weeks or days to live), the surviving people must prepare and support each other during the crisis of death. The death of an individual is by itself a moving and huge step in the life of the survivors. If possible, the passing must be expected and planned... *when I die, I want to be buried on the hill near the tree, or spread my ashes off the fishing pier, etc.* The person departing wants to know his life had meaning, and his loved ones know how much he cared and was cared for. There are volumes written on this topic of preparation for death and the effects on the survivors. A group hug does wonders when it comes to emotional support for the survivors. This support is essential in getting through the funeral, the realization of the loss, and the aftermath of being alone and missing your partner. Friends, family, church members, and acquaintances contribute to easing the pain of the loss. It is not an easy accomplishment for the spouse or children, but with time and prayer living becomes easier, and life has a meaning and purpose. Whether it's to become a better individual in the memory of that loved one or striving to contribute to the social development of your neighborhood, you will find a purpose to re-energize yourself and family members for a common goal.

My wife's cousin recently lost her husband, SWAT Entry Team Leader Craig "Metal" Meyer, Chief of Police for the Township of Bedminster, New Jersey. That man had a purpose every day for the police officers under his command, for his community, his associates, and his wife and son. He loved them all, and it showed in all he accomplished for the New Jersey areas he served. His eulogies and ceremony were the most memorable display of comradeship and devotion by his family and professional associates, including supporting counties and state organizations, ever witnessed. Along with the support of the SWAT team brothers informing his son and wife that "his brothers are there for each of them," the team is also there for each other.

This service was an open display of love and support by all and for all directly affected by the passing of "Metal." It was a celebration of his life that included three varied and loving eulogies, a military drill team, rifle salutes, bagpipers, a US flag presentation, the squawk box calling for the commander's attention with no response and eventually declaring no contact with, "Metal, stand down—never to be forgotten," and a New Jersey State Police helicopter flyover prior to the departure of the ashes in the SWAT BearCat vehicle. Every move was made with precision, love, and dedication to a fallen comrade. The survivors have an incredible foundation to recall "Metal" and to reestablish their own lives while living with a tremendous loss and void of this loved one, Craig Meyer. RIP, sir.

There are survivors every day who are mentally absent from active life. Their depression must be subdued, and they must be brought back to reality with help from trained individuals. Their pain is real. Death and cancer are cruel. By being a survivor, you cheat death and prevail in life. Life needs a buddy system, and together the survivors win.

#######

EPILOGUE

I Wish You Enough

Recently, I overheard a father and daughter in their last moments together at the airport. They had announced the departure.

Standing near the security gate they hugged, and the Father said, "I love you, and I wish you enough."

The daughter replied, "Dad, our life together has been more than enough. Your love is all I ever needed. I wish you enough too, Dad."

They kissed, and the daughter left. The father walked over to the window where I was seated. Standing there I could see he wanted and needed to cry. I tried not to intrude on his privacy, but he welcomed me in by asking, "Did you ever say good-bye to someone knowing it would be forever?"

"Yes, I have," I replied. "Forgive me for asking, but why is this a for-ever good-bye?",
"I am old, and she lives so far away. I have challenges ahead, and the reality is the next trip back will be for my funeral," he said.

"When you were saying good-bye, I heard you say, 'I wish you enough.' May I ask what that means?"

He began to smile. "That's a wish that has been handed down from other generations. My parents used to say it to everyone..." He paused a moment and looked up as if trying to remember it in detail, and he smiled even more. "When we said, 'I wish you enough,' we were wanting the other person to have a life filled with just enough good things to sustain them." Then turning toward me, he shared the following as if he were reciting it from memory.

"I wish you enough sun to keep your attitude bright no matter how gray the day may appear.
I wish you enough rain to appreciate the sun even more.
I wish you enough happiness to keep your spirit alive and everlasting.
I wish you enough pain so that even the smallest of joys in life may appear bigger.
I wish you enough gain to satisfy your wanting.
I wish you enough loss to appreciate all that you possess.
I wish you enough hellos to get you through the final good-bye."

He then began to cry and walked away.

They say it takes a minute to find a special person, an hour to appreciate them, a day to love them, but then an entire life to forget them.

TAKE TIME TO LIVE....

To all my friends and loved ones, **I WISH YOU ENOUGH.**

"I wish you enough"
By Bob Perks
Used with permission
http://www.bobperks.com/

For additional information or speaking engagements, please contact me at:

Jim Serritella
301-253-3600
8004 Hilton Road
Laytonsville, MD 20882
jim@ezstitches.com

===================== Z Z Z Z Z =====================

CPSIA information can be obtained at www.ICGtesting.com
Printed in the USA
BVOW01s0556230816

459274BV00008B/17/P